J A W L E N S K Y

NORTON SIMON MUSEUM

CHILD WITH DOLL, c. 1910
Oil on cardboard, 27¼ x 20⅛″

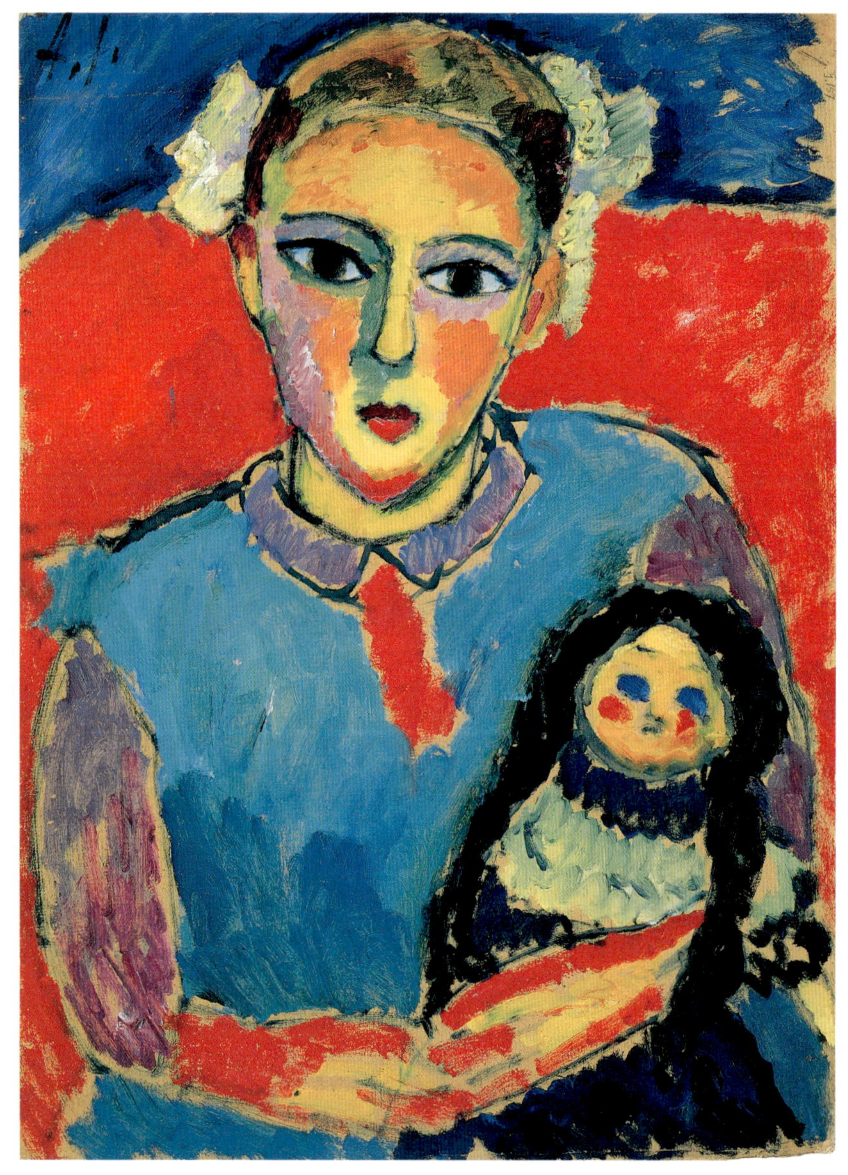

ALEXEI JAWLENSKY

Alexei Jawlensky was born in Russia in 1864. Although he is most frequently identified with the German Expressionist painters, he never aligned himself exclusively with any twentieth century stylistic movement. Instead he perfected a highly personal form influenced heavily by his deep religious convictions and a strong attraction to the mysticism of the Eastern Orthodox Church.

At the age of sixteen Jawlensky visited his first art exhibit. "I was so deeply affected," he recalled, "that it was a case of Saul becoming Paul. It was the turning point of my life. Ever since then art has been my ideal, my holy of holies, that for which my soul and my entire self yearn."[1] That "turning point" led Jawlensky to produce some of the most powerful and spiritual paintings of the twentieth century. However, it was another sixteen years before he could fully devote himself to this calling.

As the son of a colonel in the Russian Imperial Army, Jawlensky had been expected to continue the family's service to the military in spite of his enthusiastic interest in painting. He complied by attending military school and was commissioned a lieutenant in the army when he was twenty. Nevertheless, at his first opportunity he attended evening courses at the Imperial Art Academy in St. Petersburg. There he met the leading Russian realist painter Ilya Repin, who introduced him to a circle of artists which included the painter Marianne von Werefkin. In 1896 Jawlensky resigned his commission as captain in the army and with Werefkin left Russia to study art in Munich. He was to live the rest of his life in Germany and Switzerland.

In Munich Jawlensky enrolled in the painting class of Yugoslav artist Anton Ažbè. A popular and generous teacher, Ažbè believed that color was the fundamental means of modeling forms, and emphasized the use of pure, unmixed colors applied directly to the canvas.[2] It was in Ažbè's studio that Jawlensky began his lifelong friendship with a fellow Russian, Wassily Kandinsky.

The next decade was one of enormous creative activity; he travelled widely in France and Italy and participated in exhibitions in Germany and Russia. At the urging of the ballet impresario Diaghilev, Jawlensky exhibited ten works in the 1905 *Salon d'Automne* in Paris. He came under the influence of Gauguin, Cézanne, van Gogh, and Matisse in particular, while developing his own very personal style.

Jawlensky and Werefkin spent the summers of 1908 and 1909 with Kandinsky and the artist Gabrielle Munter in Murnau, a village about 40 miles south of Munich. The work of both Kandinsky and Jawlensky during the Murnau period is characterized by flat areas of bright, pure colors, outlined, mosaic fashion, with contrasting colors.

In January 1909 Jawlensky and Kandinsky, along with other artists and intellectuals, founded their own independent artists' organization, The New Artists' Association of Munich (*Neue Künstlervereinigung, or NKV*). Three exhibitions followed from 1909 to

1912, and attracted international artists such as Braque, Picasso, Rouault and Vlaminck. Under Kandinsky's direction, the Association became a showcase for modern art. The artist Franz Marc noted in the *Blue Rider Almanac* in 1912 that "In Munich the first and only serious representatives of the new ideas were two Russians who had lived there for many years and who had worked quietly until some Germans joined them."[3] Kandinsky left the group in 1911, Jawlensky a year later.

Shortly after the outbreak of World War I, Jawlensky fled to Switzerland, settling in St. Prex on Lake Geneva. There he began his "Variations on a Landscape Theme," painting a profusion of compositions inspired by the view from his window.[4] In 1916 he began a life-long friendship with Emmy (Galka) Scheyer, who gave up her own painting career to devote herself to furthering that of Jawlensky. Scheyer organized a successful exhibition of Jawlensky's work in Wiesbaden in 1921, but financial trouble plagued the artist as Europe's economy collapsed. In 1922 he returned to Germany and settled permanently in Wiesbaden. After his resettlement in Germany, and for the remainder of his life, he concentrated almost exclusively on depicting the human face.

Jawlensky was stricken with arthritis in 1929, which became progressively more severe and more painful. "If only I didn't have such persistent pain," he wrote, "...I paint by holding the brush in both hands and the palette resting with one end on the easel and with the other on my knees."[5] The Nazis forbade the exhibition of Jawlensky's works, and in 1937 included his paintings in the Nazi-sponsored "Exhibition of Degenerate Art" in Munich. A year later he ceased to paint because of the paralyzing effects of his disease. Jawlensky died in March, 1941, in Wiesbaden.

In 1924 Galka Scheyer had organized The Blue Four, a group of artists which included Jawlensky, Paul Klee, Lionel Feininger and Wassily Kandinsky, with herself as their representative. She came to America to promote the work of the Blue Four, writing, lecturing, and organizing exhibitions until her death in 1945. Scheyer's bequest of over 450 works of art and 800 documents constitutes The Blue Four Galka Scheyer Collection at the Norton Simon Museum.

Sara Campbell Abdo
Chief Curator

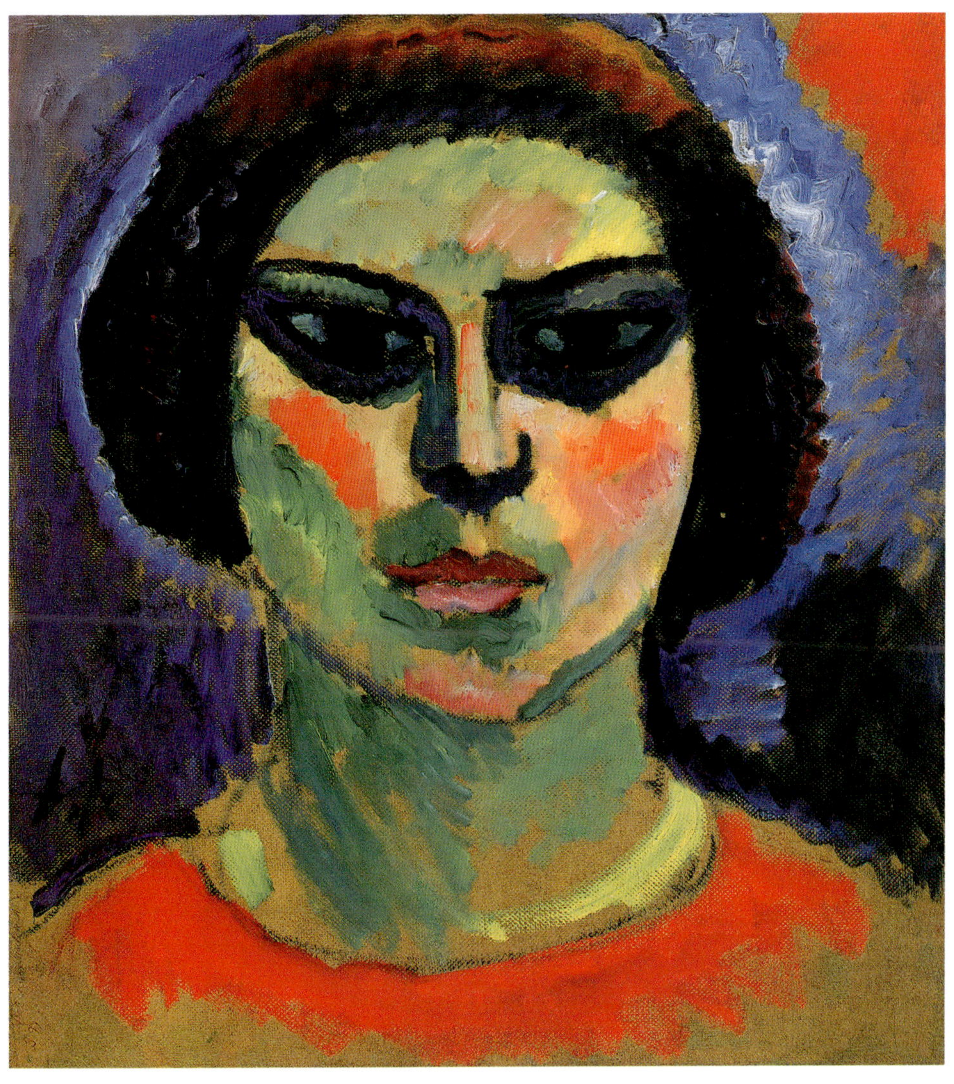

BLOSSOMING GIRL, c. 1911
Oil on linen-finish paper, mounted on
canvas, 21$\frac{1}{8}$ x 19$\frac{5}{8}$"

BLONDE, 1911
Oil on cardboard, 21 x 19⅜"

In his engaging series of heads of 1910–1912 Jawlensky has reduced the illusion of three-dimensionality by applying broad patterns of decorative color to his backgrounds as well as to his figures. The luxurious colors, the bold brushwork and the voluptuous expression of the subject all contribute to the sensuous richness of the composition.

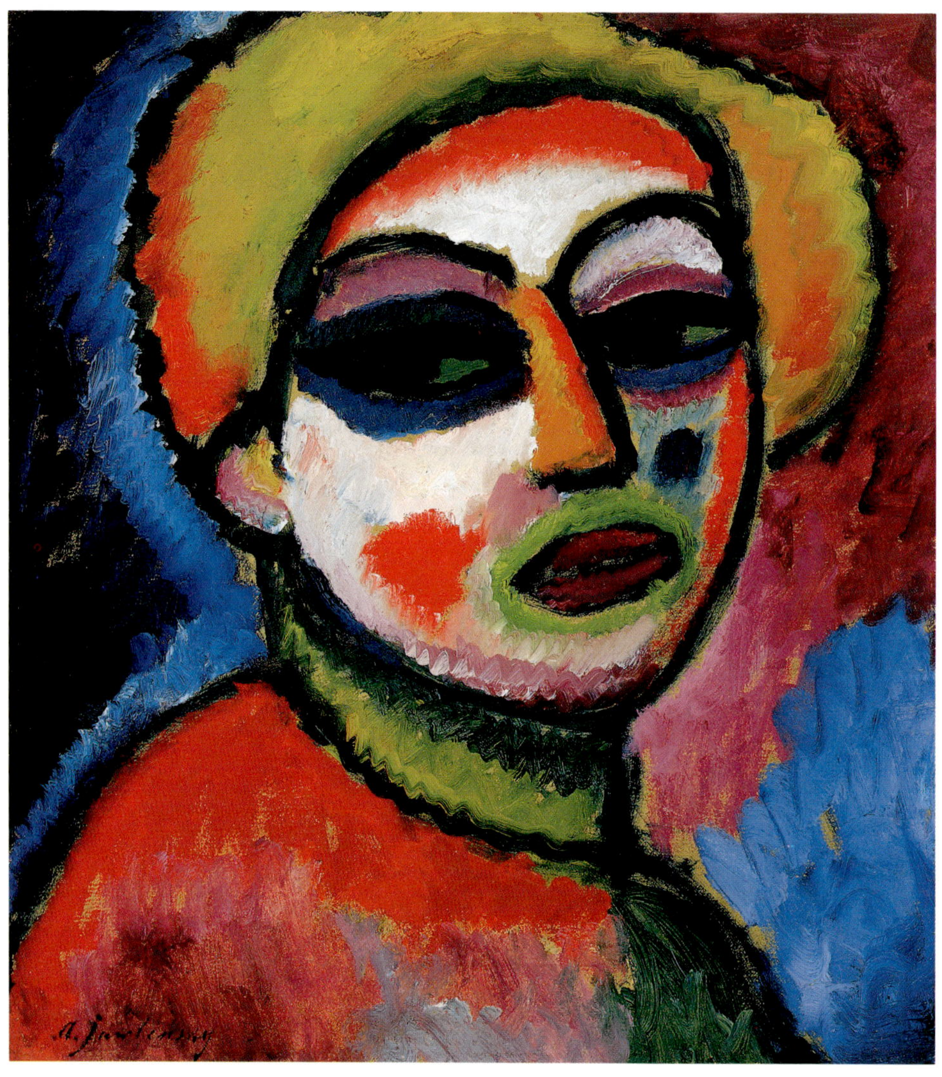

MEDITATION, 1912
Oil on linen-finish paper, mounted on
canvas, 21¼ x 19⅜″

The painted heads from this period are enclosed in small, almost square formats.
Jawlensky cut off the tops of the heads, thereby further emphasizing the faces.

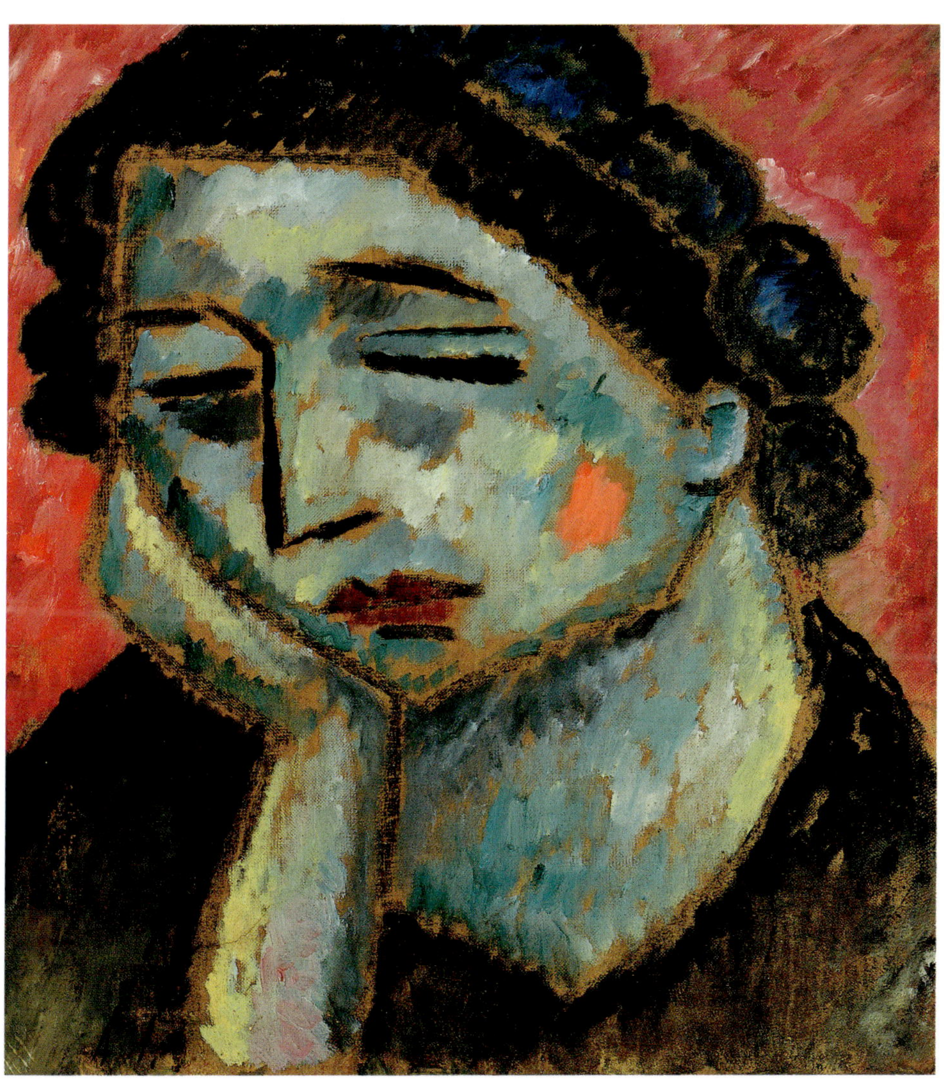

Jawlensky developed a stylization of form which moved farther away from the individual sitter and closer to an archetype. This iconography was perfected in his heads from the 1920s.

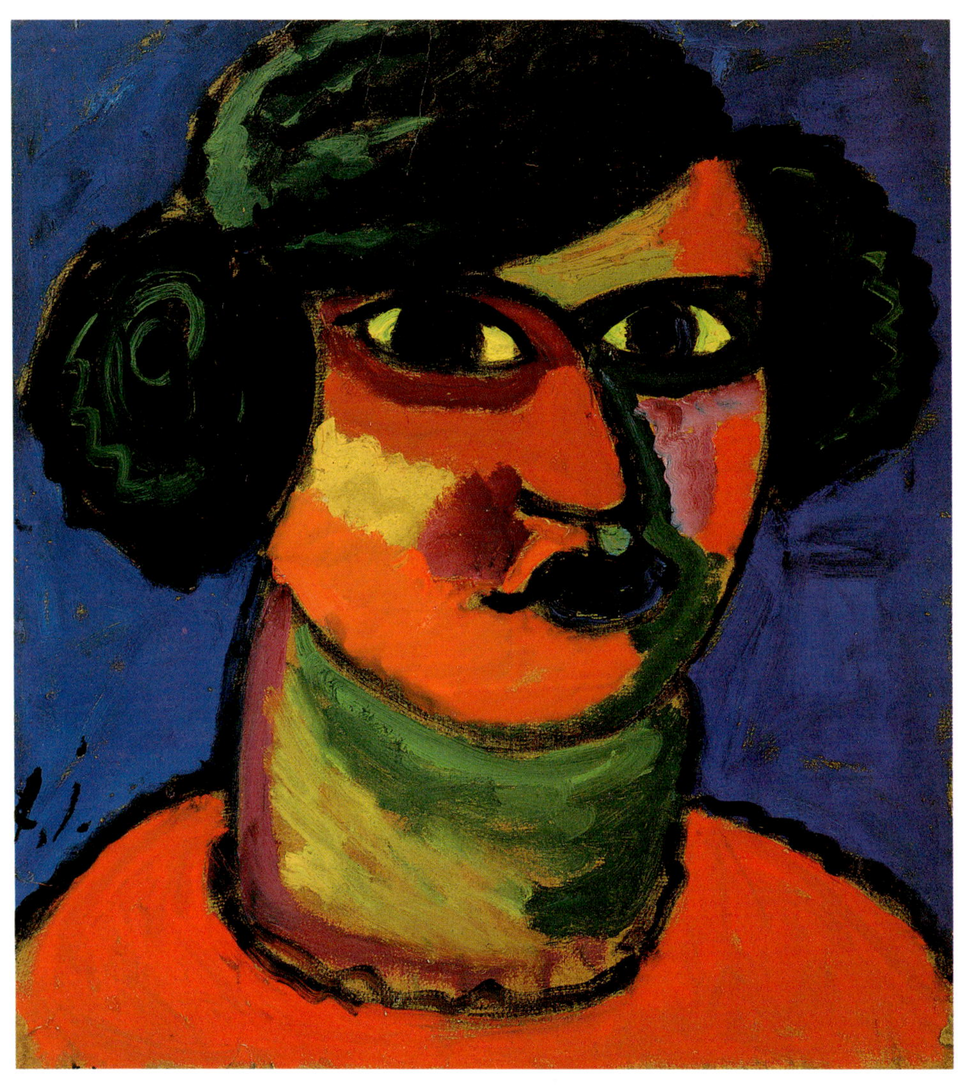

HEAD WITH WHITE OF EYES, 1912
Oil on linen-finish cardboard, 20⅞ x 19⅜"

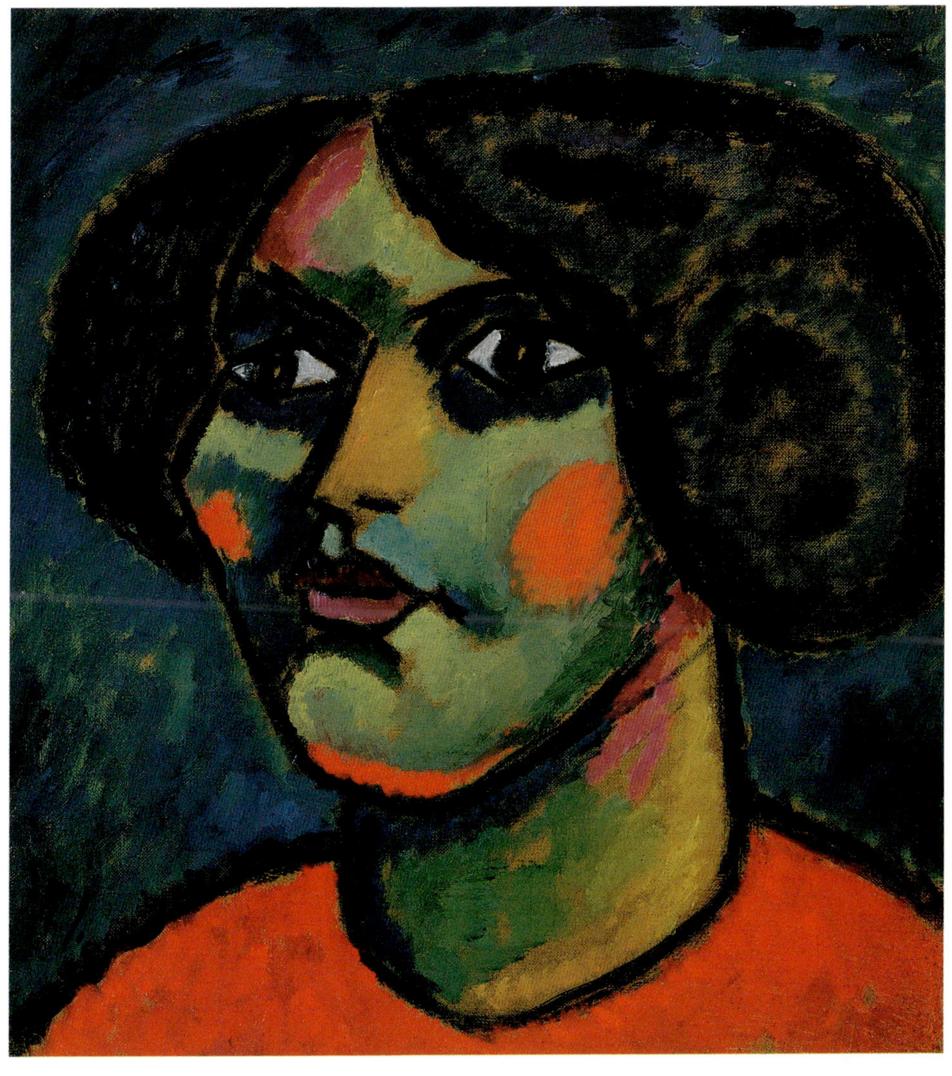

FEATHER HAT: OLGA, 1912
Oil on linen-finish paper, mounted on
canvas, 21 x 19⅝"

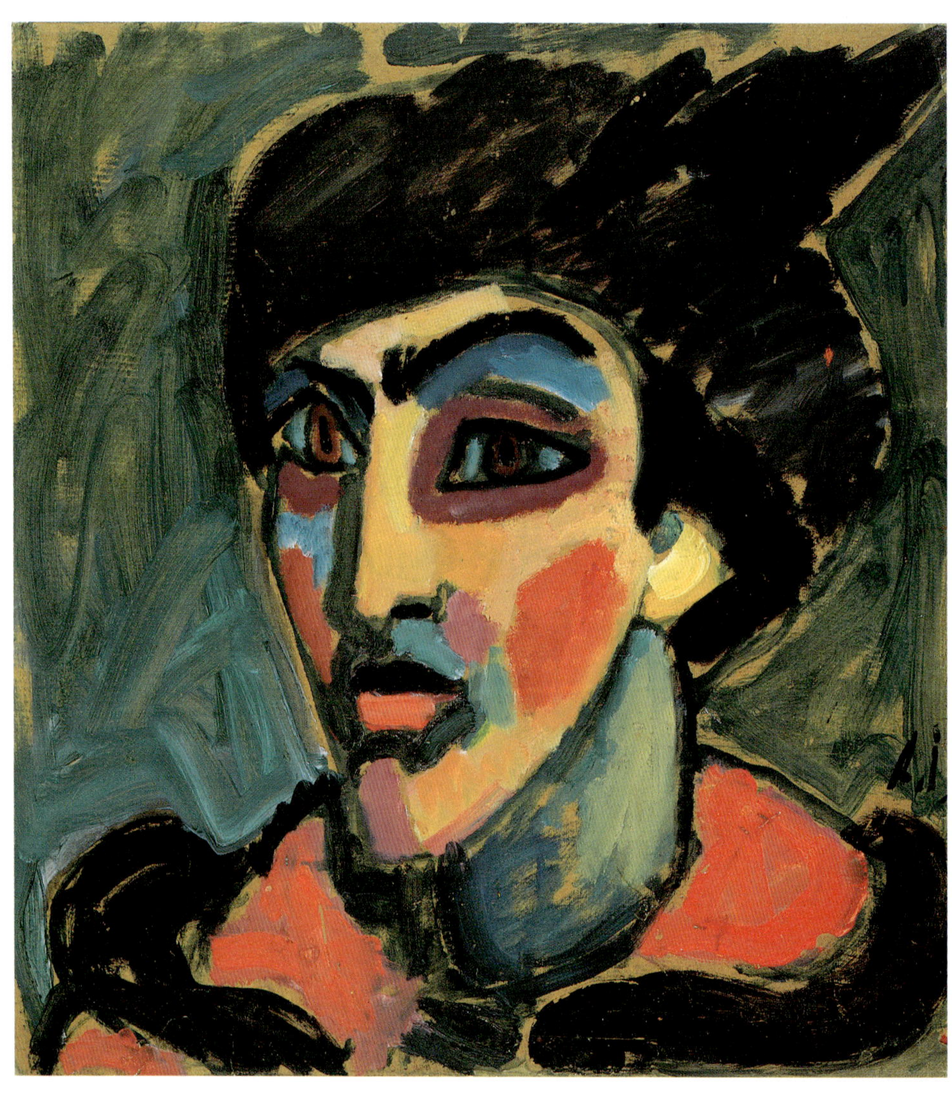

Jawlensky activated his surface with rapidly scrawled brushstrokes and delineated his shapes by enclosing them in red, blue and yellow contours.

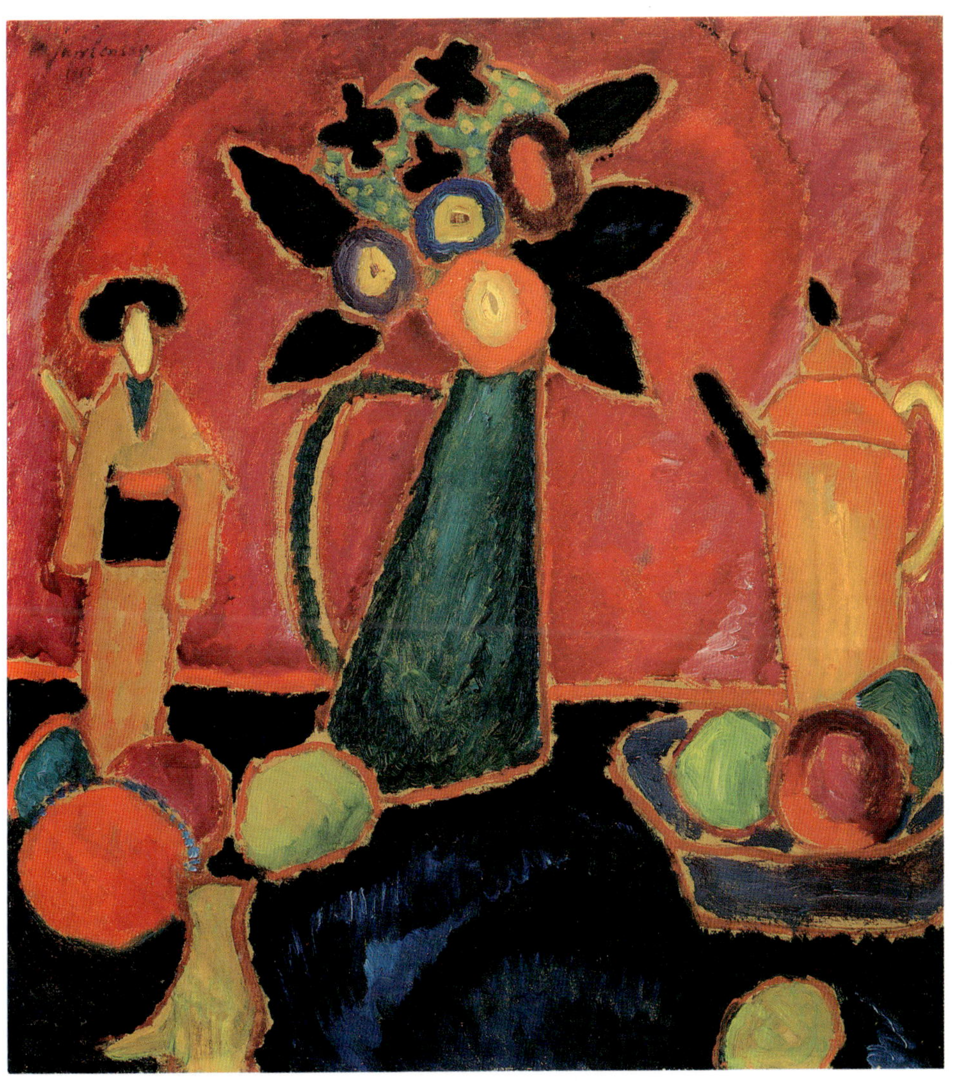

CORNFIELD, c. 1914
Oil on linen-finish paper, 10⅝ x 14⅜″

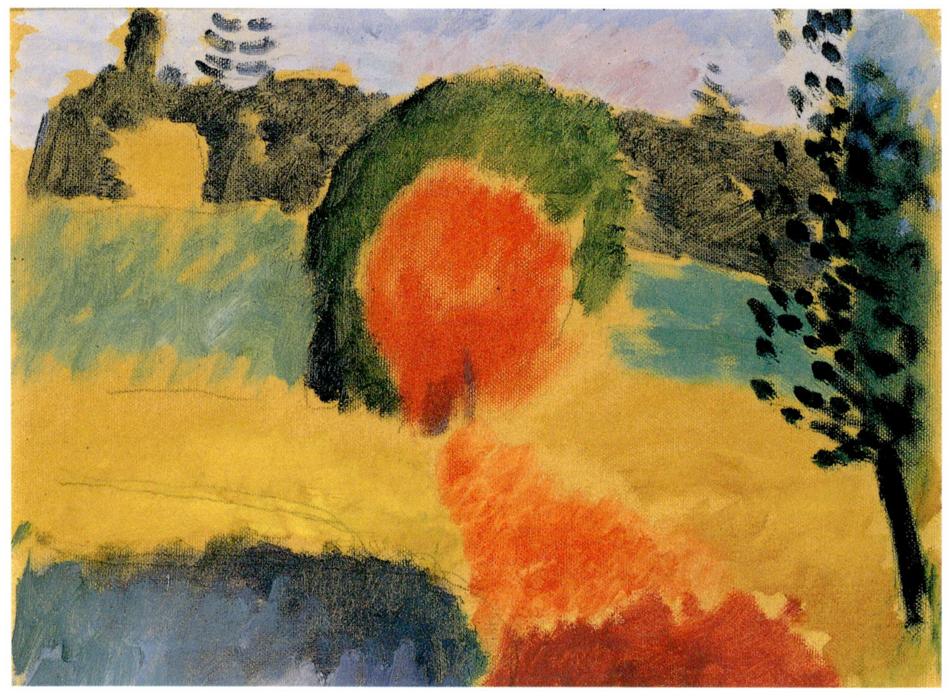

ORIENTAL CITY, 1914
Oil on cardboard, 21 x 19 ½″

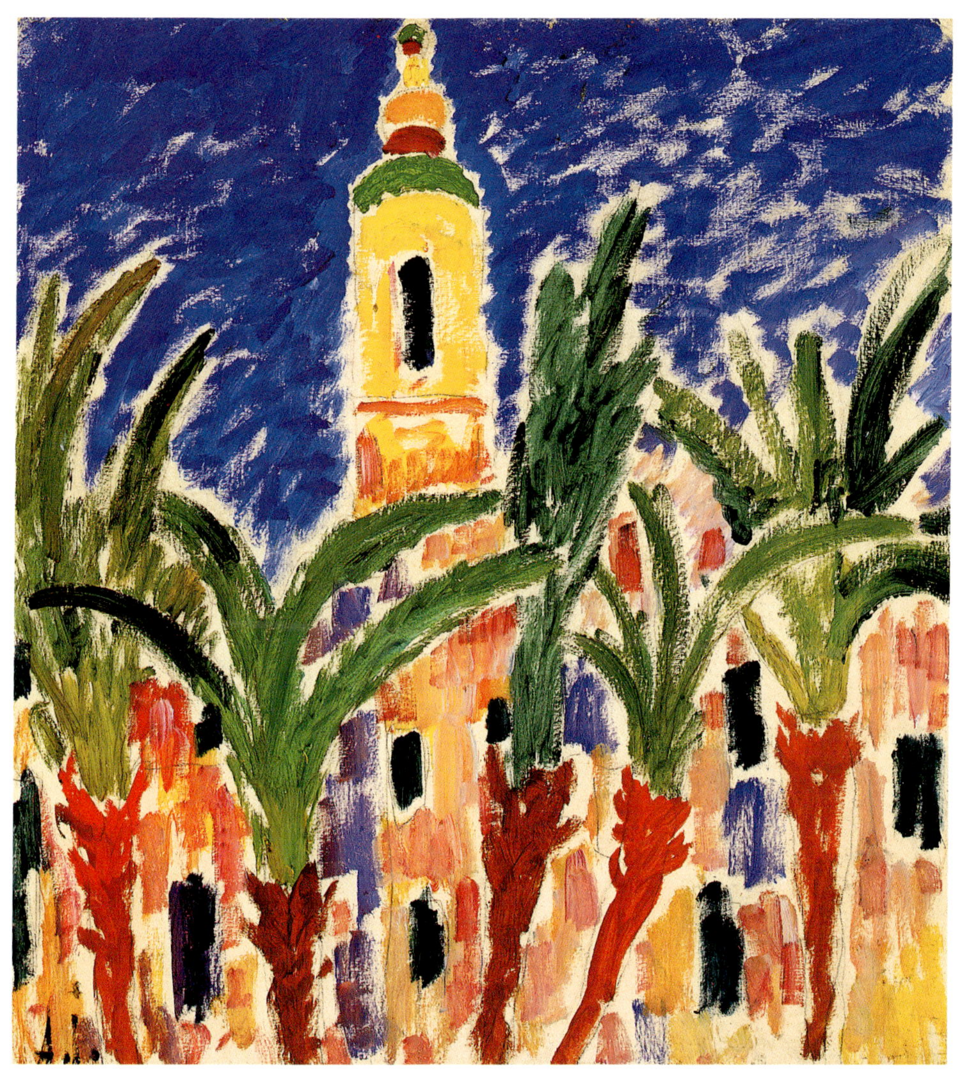

BLACK TREE: BORDIGHERA, 1914
Oil on cardboard, 21 x 19⅜″

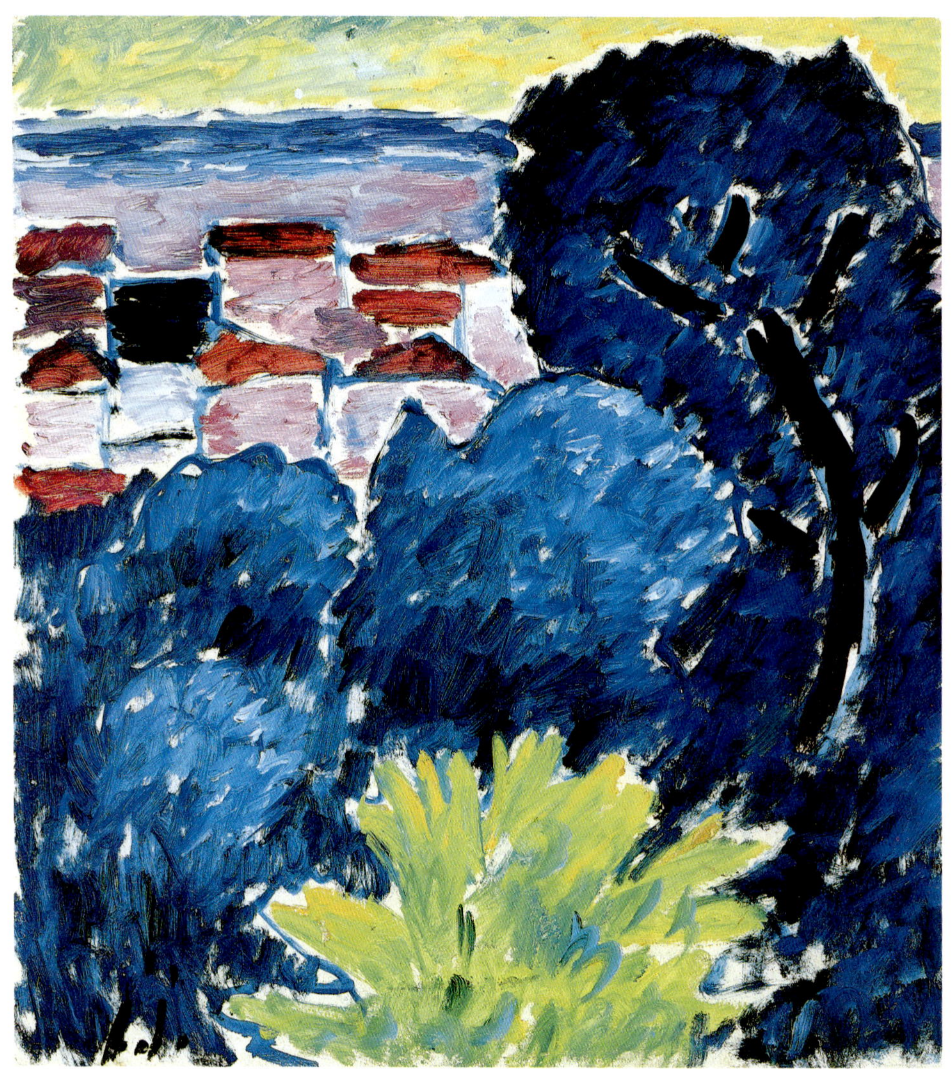

VARIATION: OURS, 1918
Oil on linen-finish paper, mounted on
cardboard, 14 3/8 x 10 3/4"

"...I have just begun a new series of Variations and thank God the beginning was good.
I am working hard and go to bed very very late. I am very nervous but not tired. My
work progresses slowly, inspiration comes, but that isn't everything—only intensive work
can bring life into my works."[6]

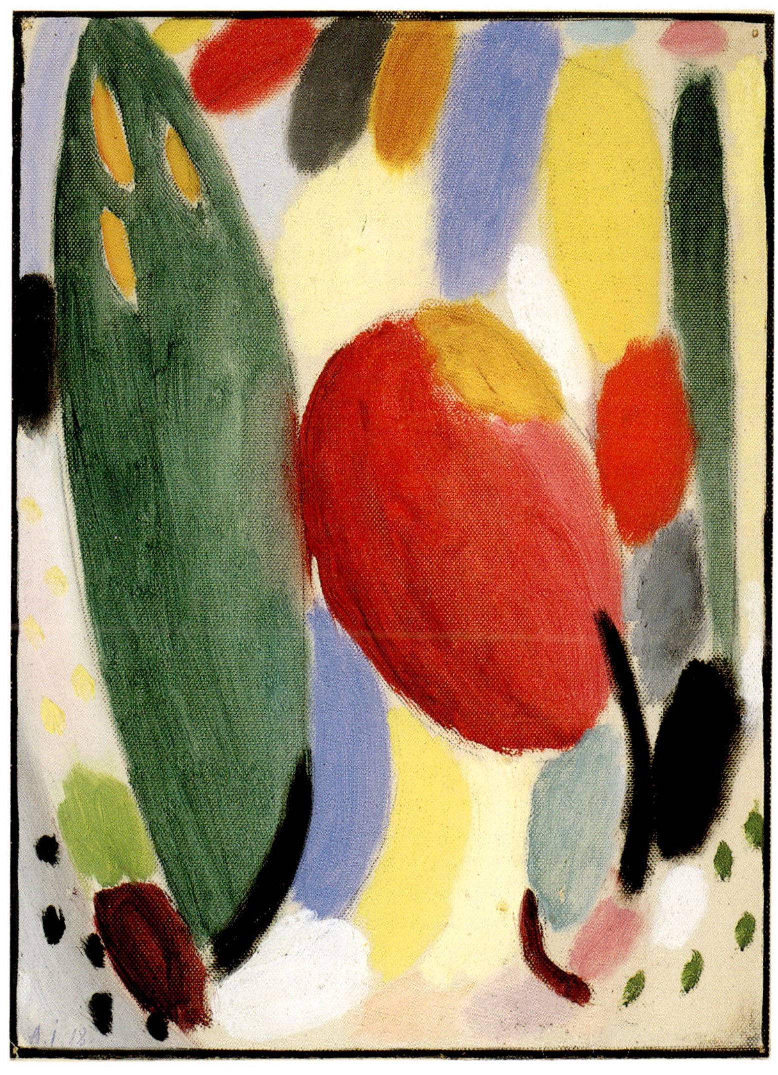

Jawlensky's "serial images" have been compared to those of Monet, who painted some thirty views of Rouen Cathedral in various weather conditions and times of day. Monet was interested in the effects of light and nature, and essentially painted what he saw. Jawlensky, on the other hand, took his inspiration from nature but did not limit himself to a literal description.

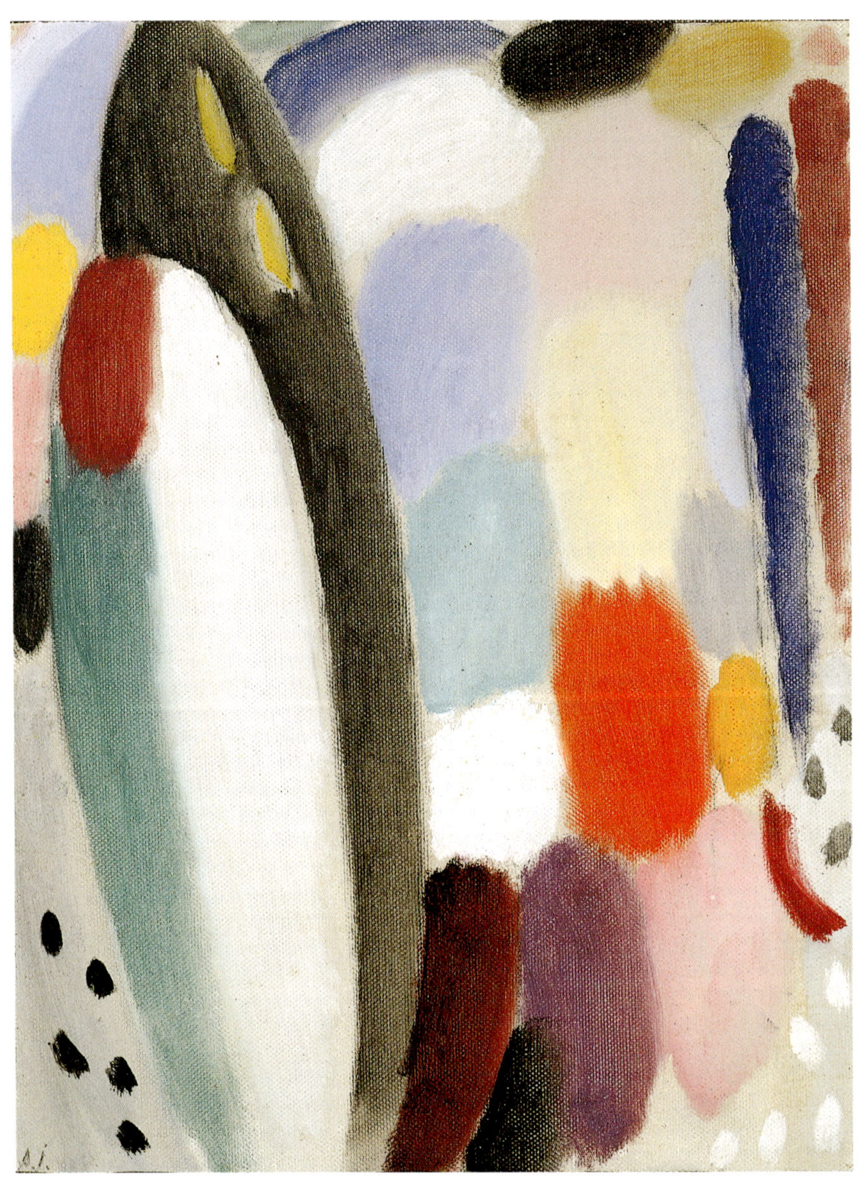

As Jawlensky tested the limits of non-objective painting, his "Variations" became more abstract. Horizons and perspective have disappeared, and color is used as a structural device rather than as a mirror of nature.

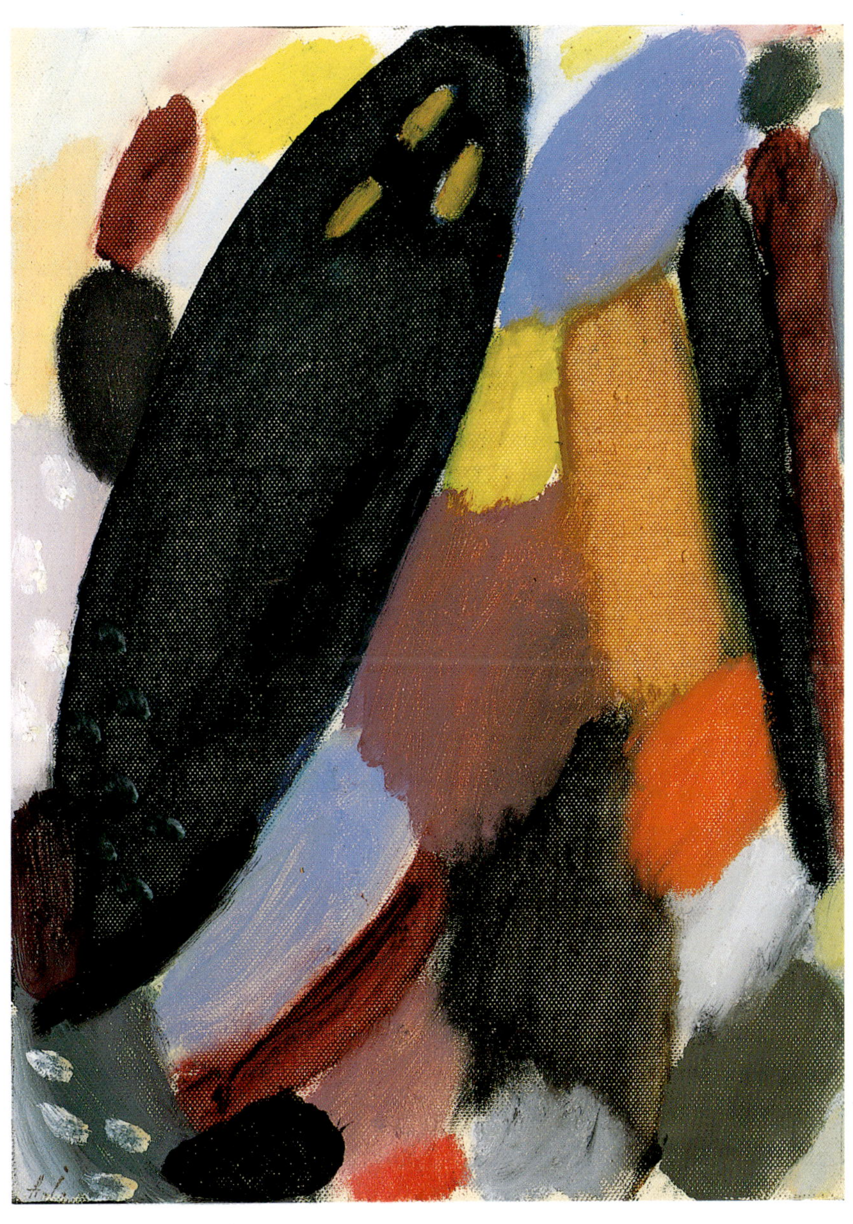

The compositional oval sweeps of the landscape "Variations," and their flat, broad color areas are still evident in Jawlensky's new series of female heads. This work is inscribed on the reverse: "To love means to live the life of him whom one loves. A. J."

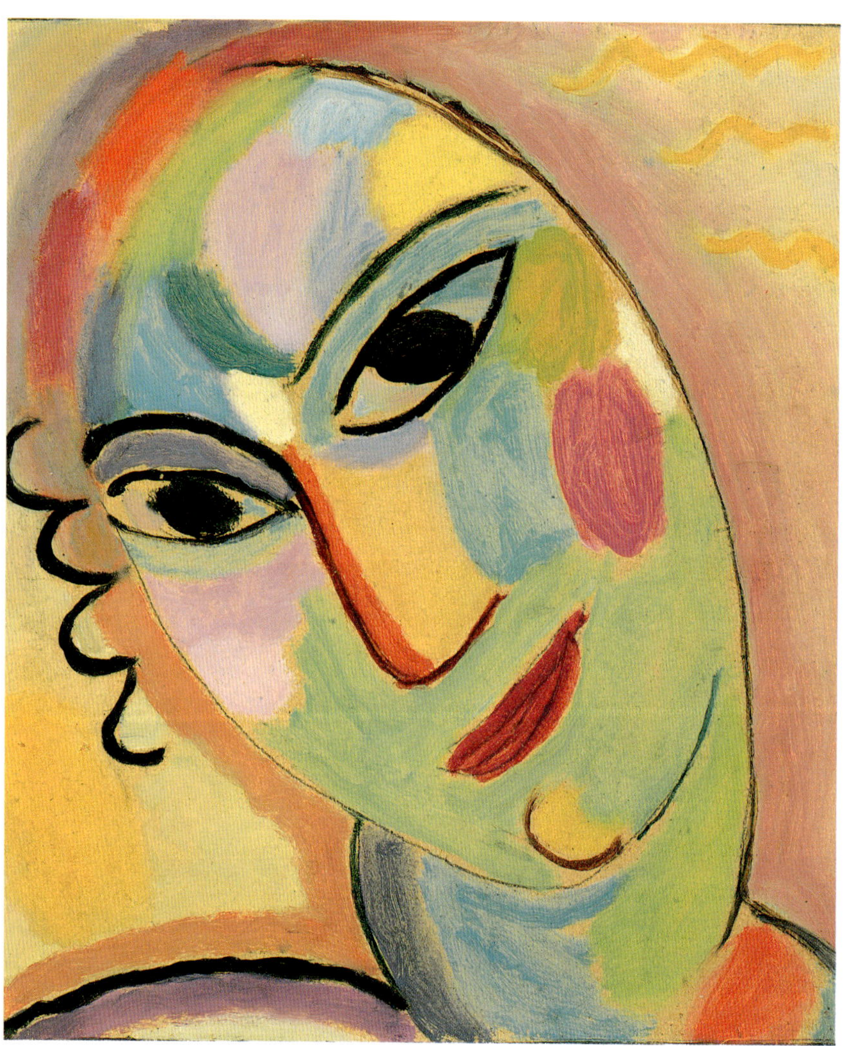

After meeting Jawlensky, Emmy Scheyer spent several months with the artist and his family in St. Prex, were she served as model for a new group of portraits. Family pressure took Scheyer back to Germany in 1919. It was during this period of separation, in December 1920, that Jawlensky wrote to Scheyer of a dream he experienced in which she appeared to him in the form of a bird.[7] From that time on, he referred to her as "Galka," the Russian word for blackbird, and it was this name which Scheyer took as her own.

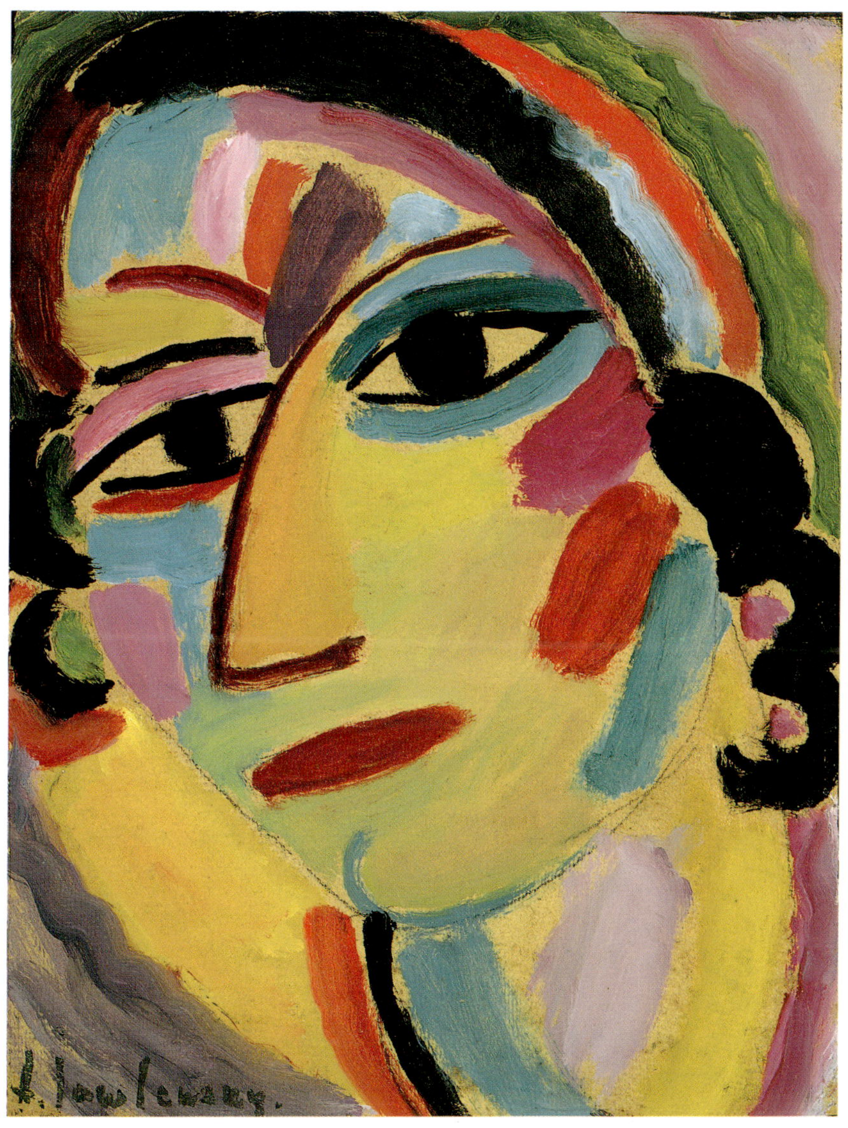

On the reverse of the painting, Jawlensky has inscribed: "If the light in you is extinguished, then a dark shadow of your own heart falls across your path. Be on guard against these terrible shadows. No light of your understanding can destroy the darknesses which flow out of your soul until all self-loving thoughts have been driven out."

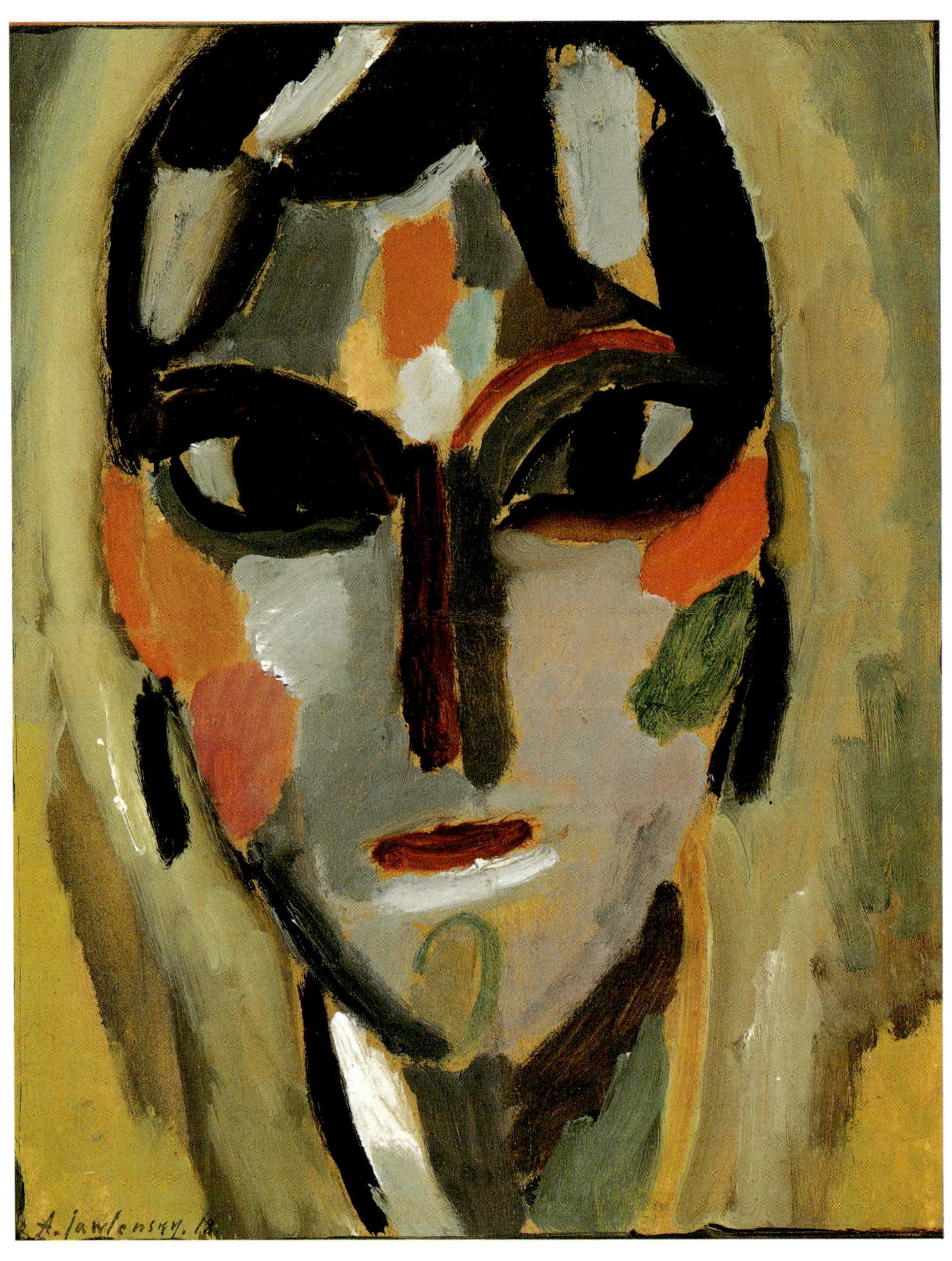

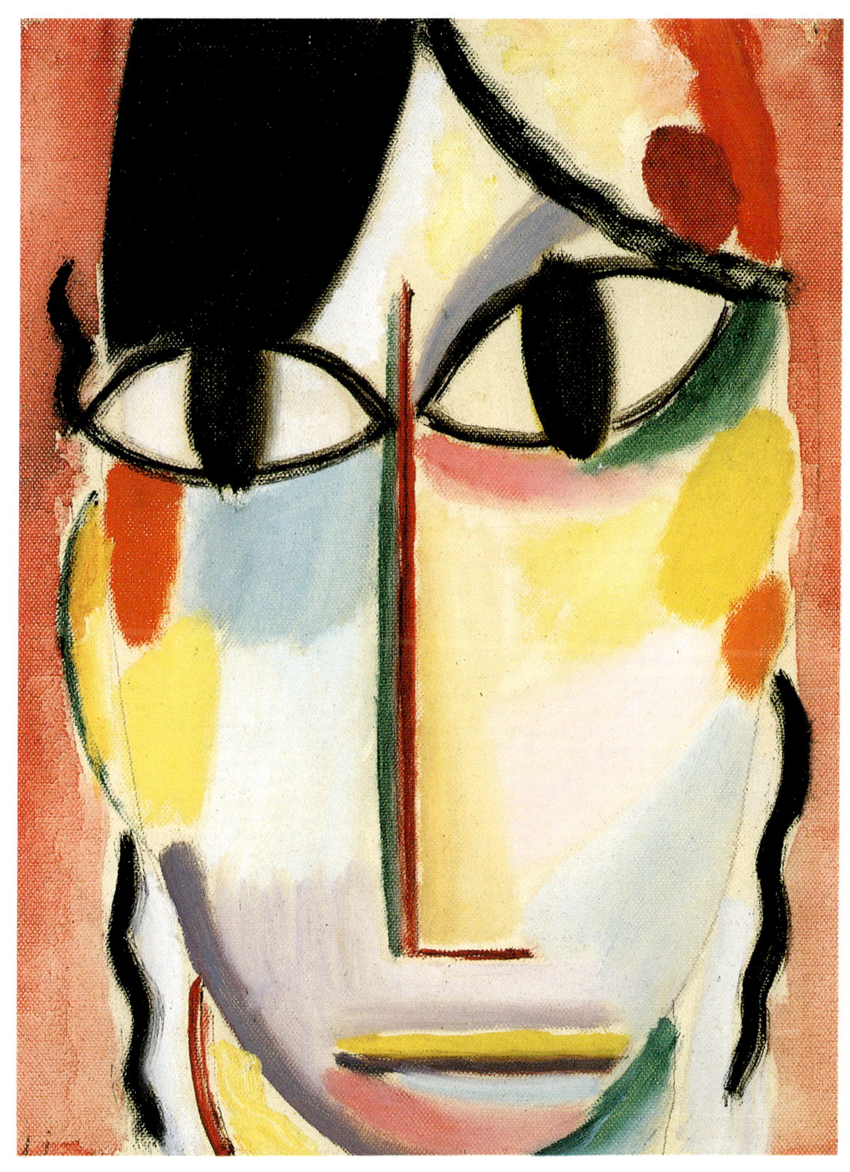

FALLEN ANGEL II, 1919
Oil on linen-finish paper, mounted on
cardboard, 14³/₈ x 10³/₄"

ASTONISHMENT, 1919
Oil on paper, mounted on cardboard, 14$\frac{1}{4}$ x 10$\frac{7}{8}$"

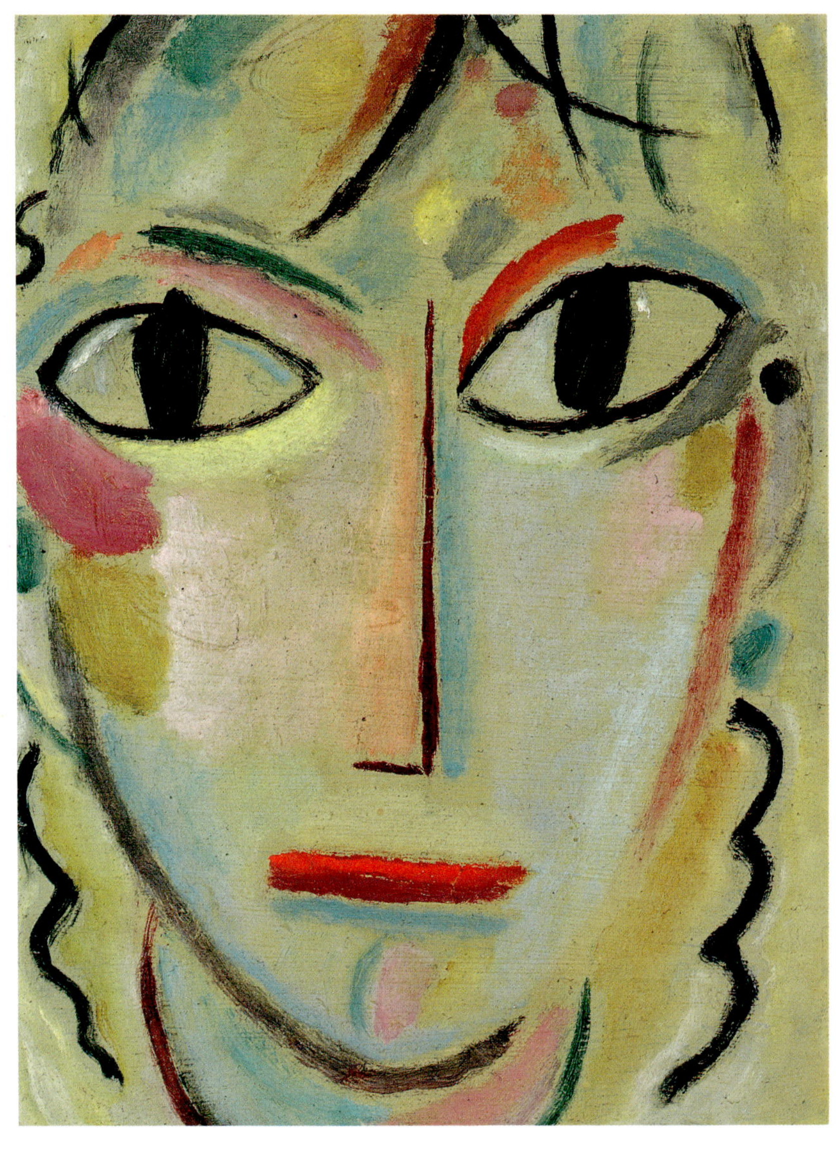

*"Yes, Kokoschka is great. But as for me! I don't want to be great and cannot be; it is
enough that I am a pure and respectable painter."*[8]

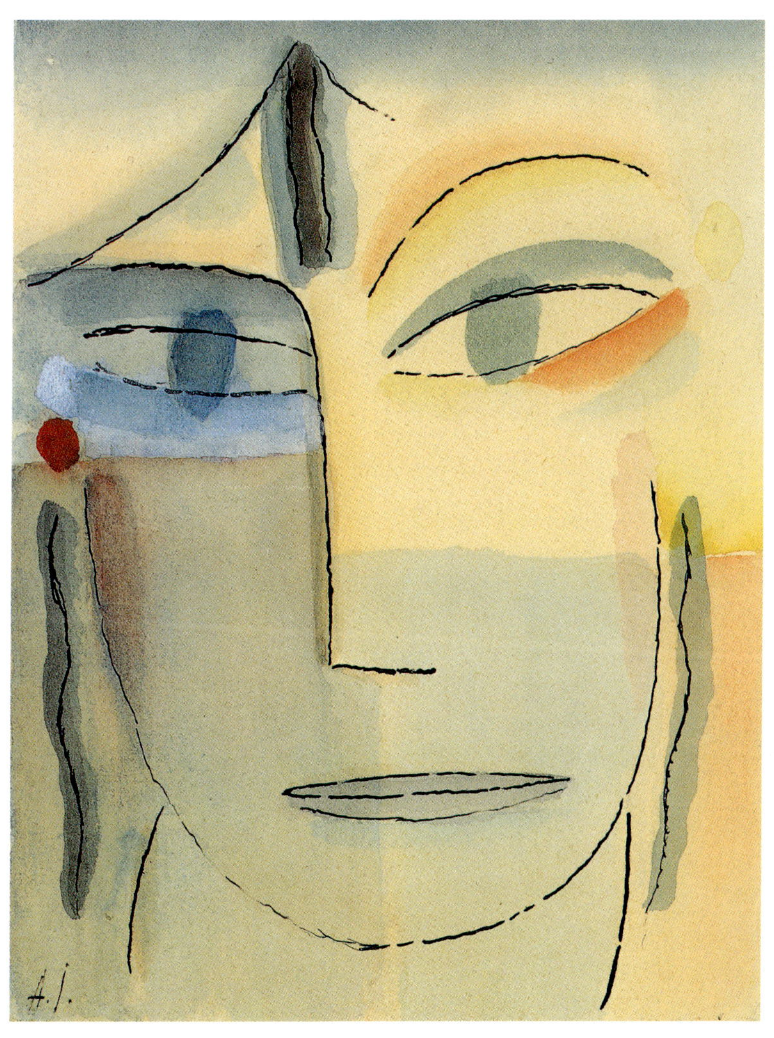

STARLIGHT, 1921
Oil on paper, mounted on cardboard, 14⅛ x 10⅝"

Jawlensky simplified his frontal views of faces until only the essential elements remain.

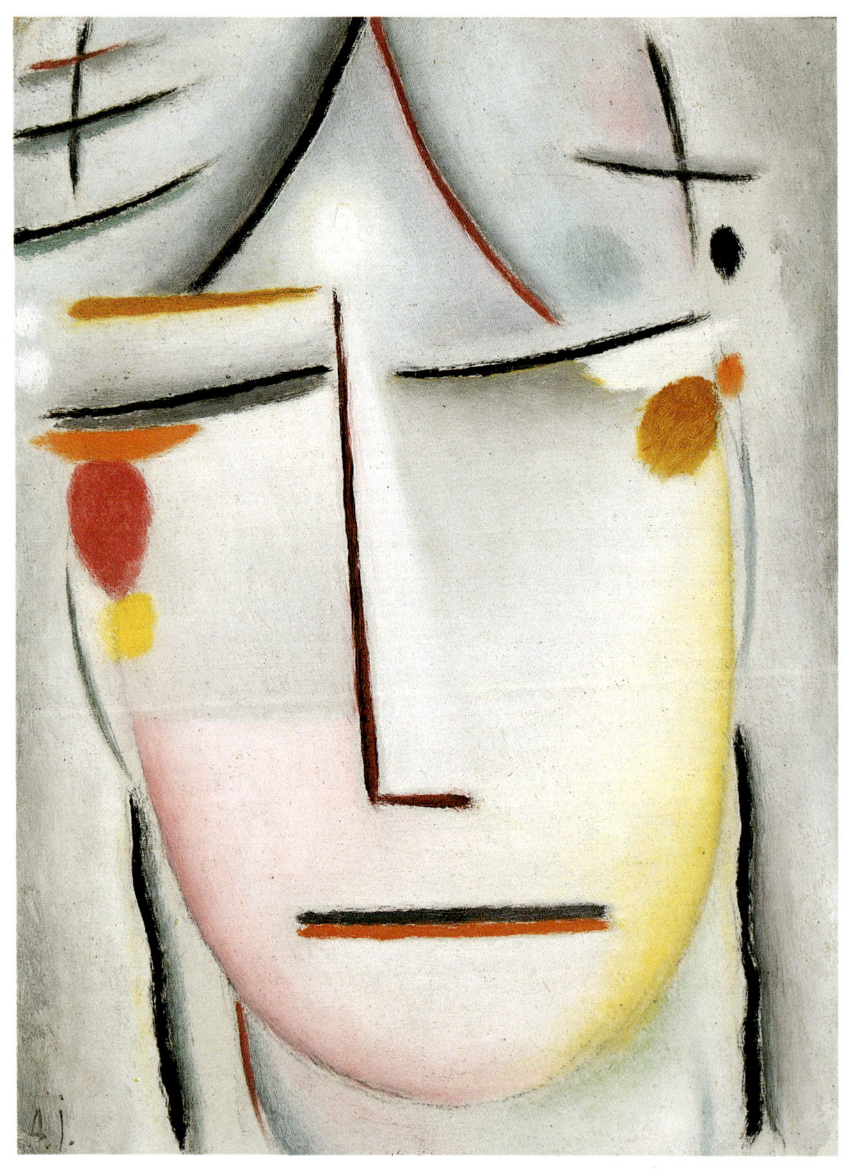

WINTER, 1921
Oil on paper, mounted on cardboard, 14 x 10⅜″

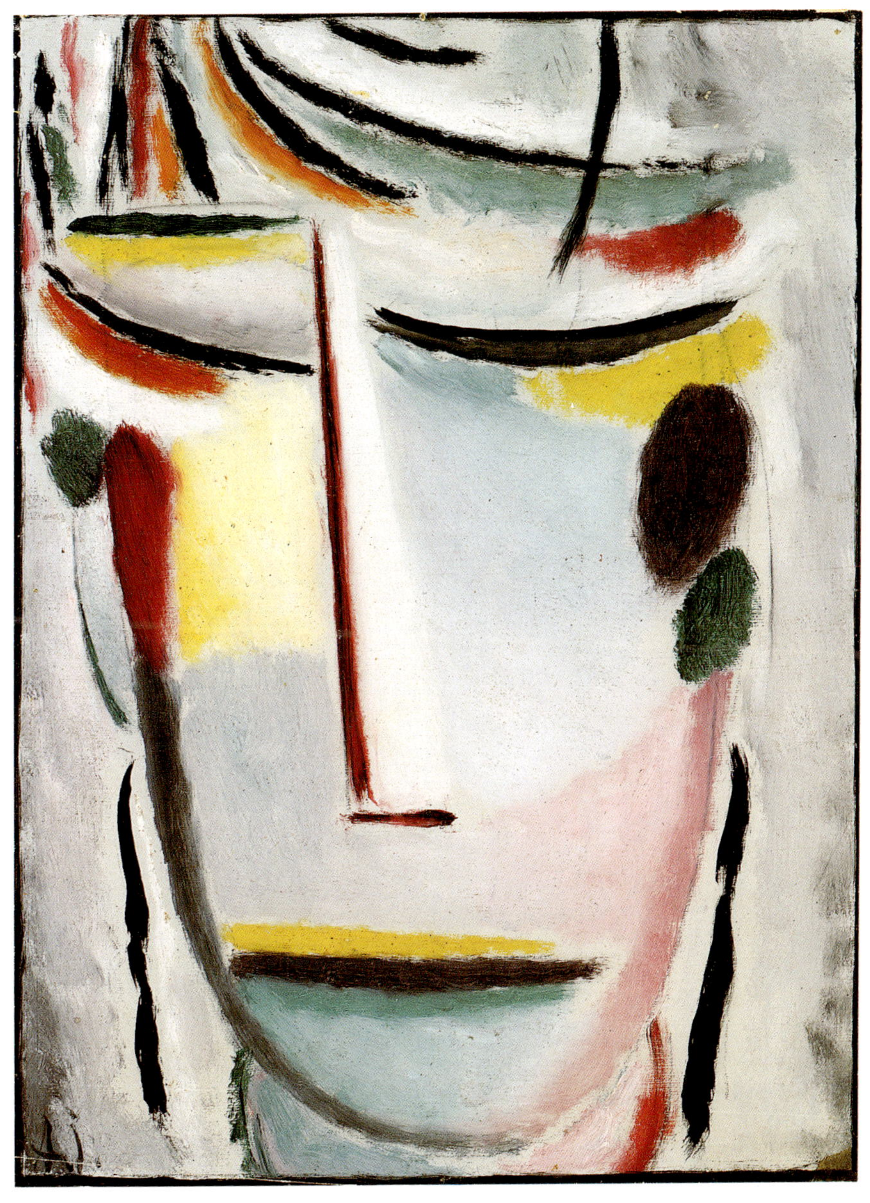

As Jawlensky explored the human face during the 1920s, he demarcated the space to the point that the boundaries did not move beyond the eyebrows, chin and ears.

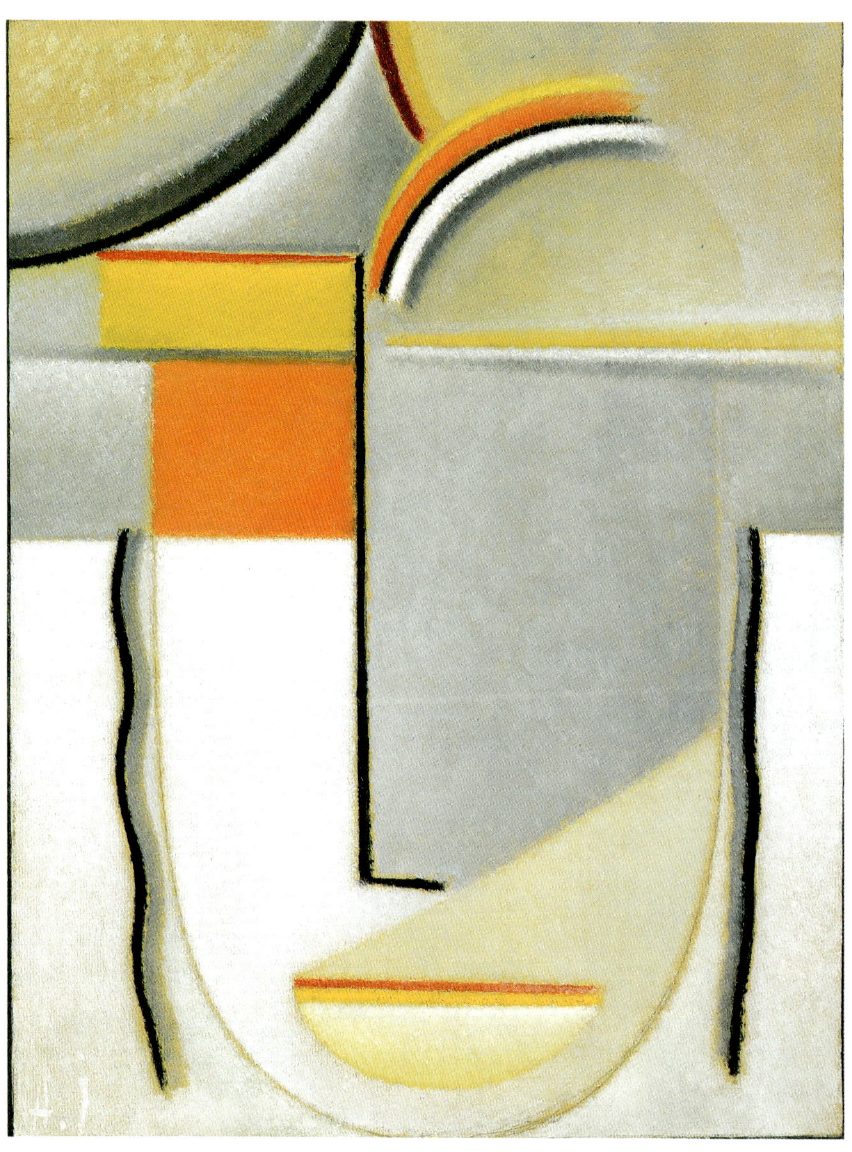

SOUNDS OF WINTER, 1927
Oil on linen-finish cardboard, 16³/₄ x 12⁷/₈"

Many writers have noted Jawlensky's progressive religious concentration upon the face during the last twenty years of his life. He shared this spiritualized view of humanity in a letter written in June 1938: "...I knew that great art should only be painted with religious feeling. And that was something I could bring only to the human face. I realized that the artist must express...that within him which is divine. That is why the work of art is a visible God, and why art is 'a longing for God.'" [9]

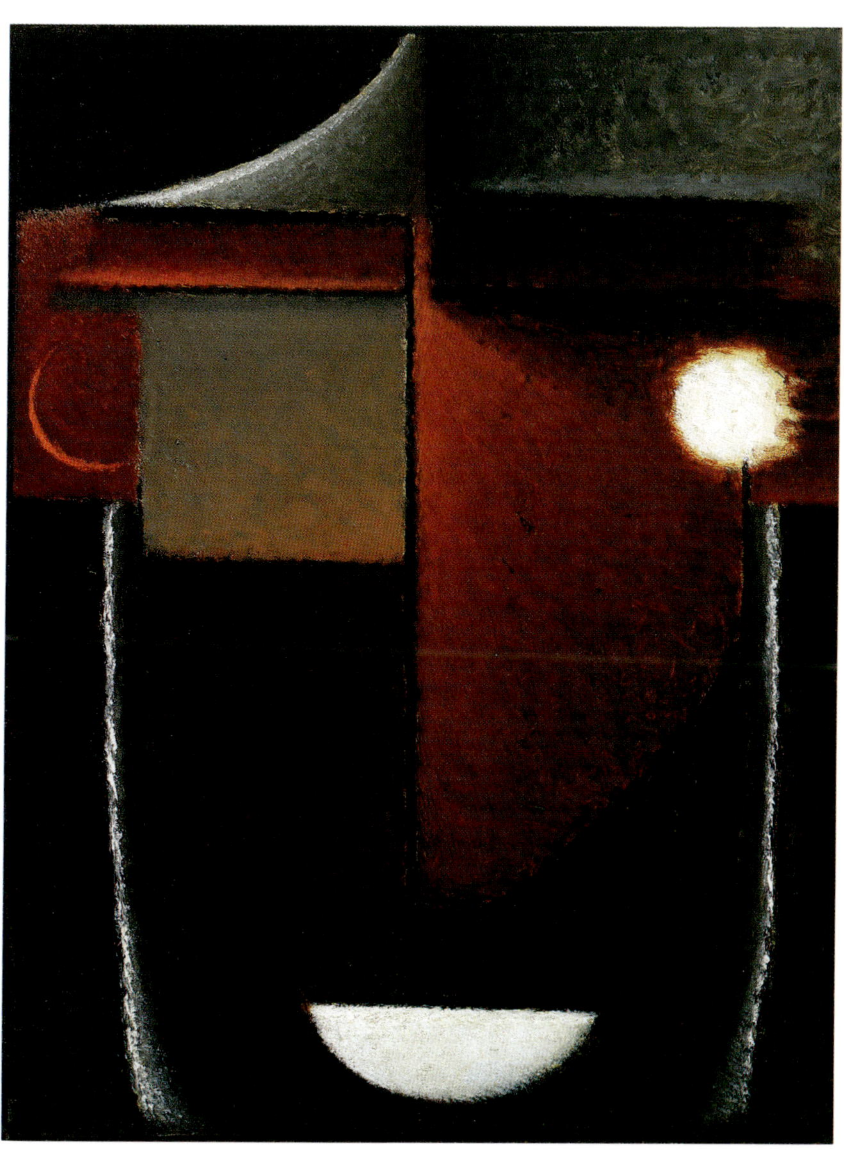

The image occurs on page one of a four-page undated letter to Scheyer, written in the fall of 1928 (erroneously dated "1929" in another hand): "My dear Galka! You are surely already in America, in San Francisco. Things are very hard for us. . . . My sketch "Hunchback" is sad. . . I have done a few good heads. And now it is so cold I freeze like a dog. . ." Jawlensky's 1911 painting "The Hunchback" was a favorite of Scheyer's, and the artist had painted a small version for her shortly after their meeting in 1917. This sketch is a remembrance of that gift.

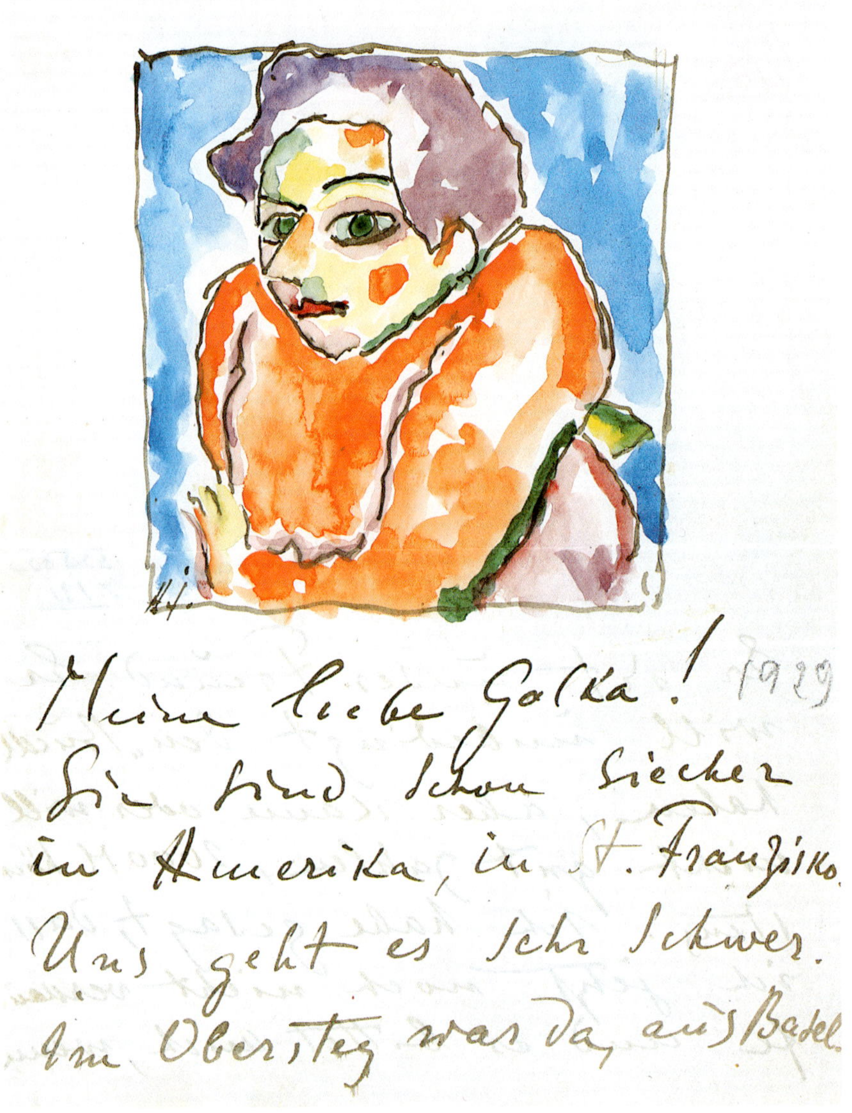

The image occurs on page one of a four-page letter to Scheyer, dated November 9, 1928, in which Jawlensky humorously prods Galka to work harder on his behalf: "...if the new President Hoover is not against art as he is against liquor, then please tell the good people over there that my art can intoxicate just like good wine, and it's not prohibited; this intoxication lasts longer, is more beautiful and healthier. Just look at the picture on the first page of this letter. It is pleading so seriously. Thus, I am asking the kind Americans to help me a little. They cannot lose. They only gain!..."

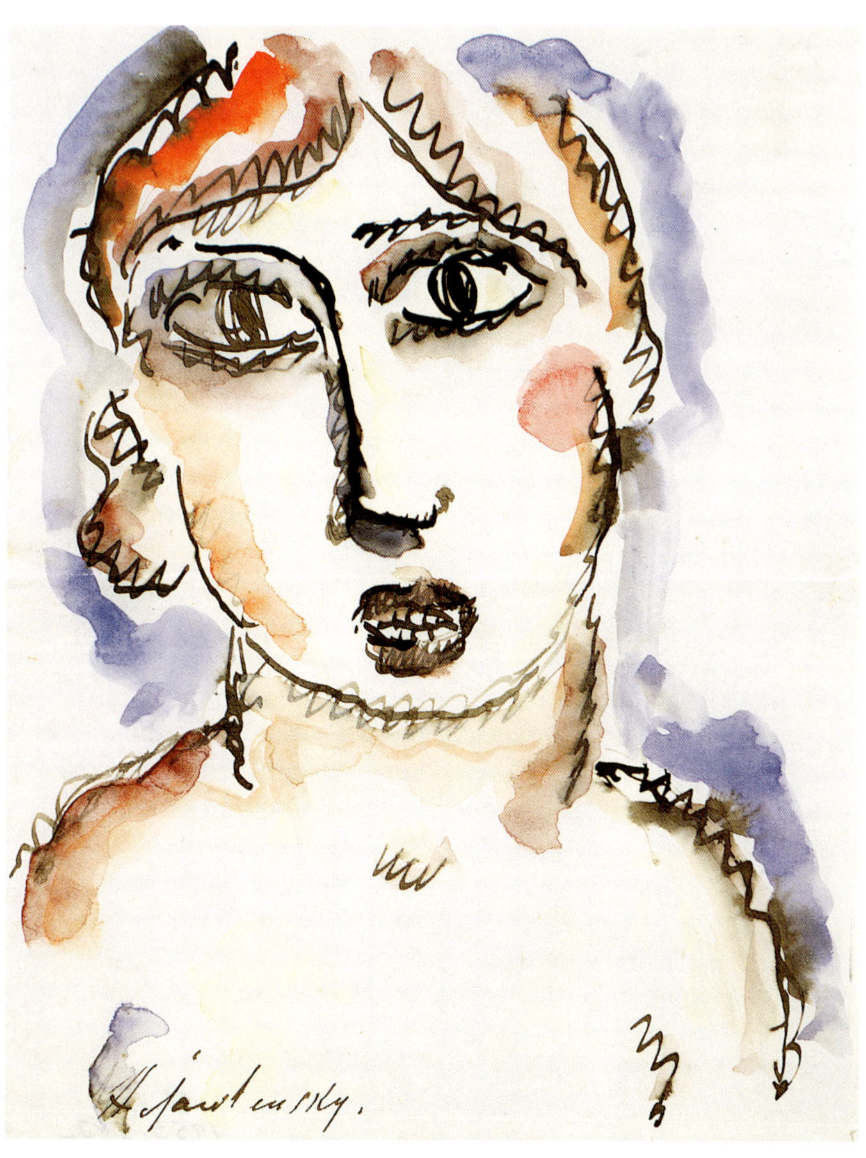

"...I am now completely absorbed in my little heads. Oh, they are so dear to me and so close to my soul; they are profound and very beautifully religious, and very concentrated in feeling...."[10]

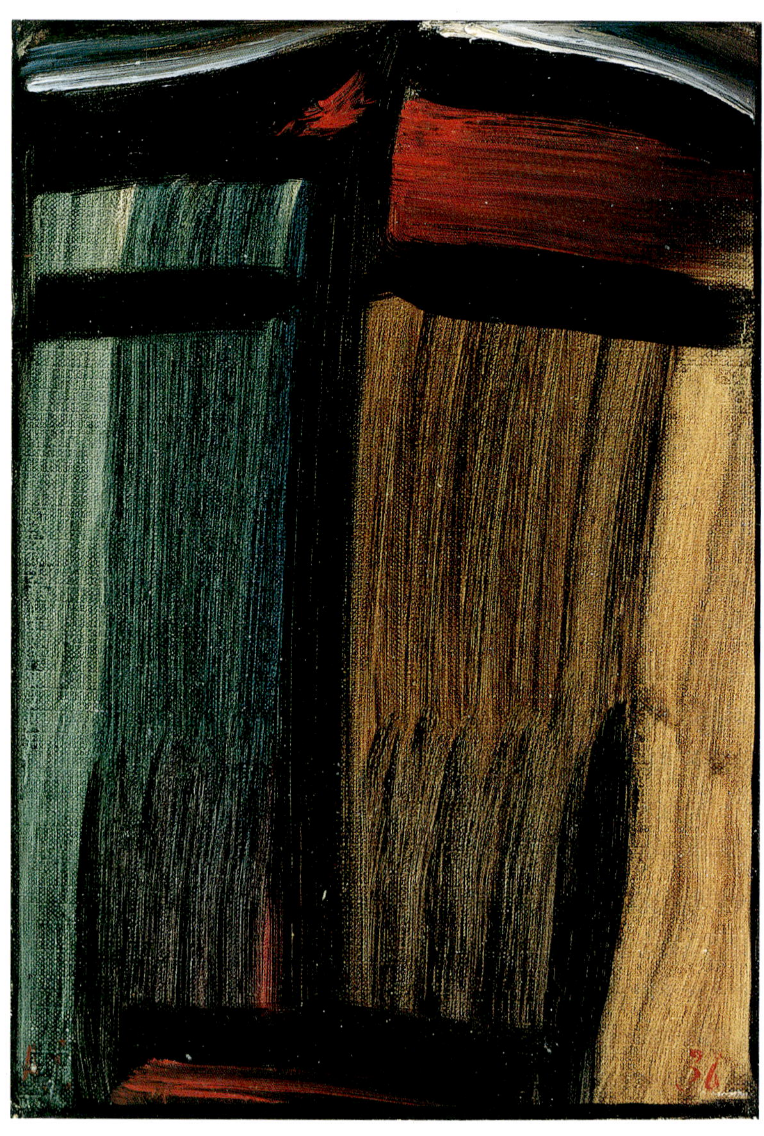

Jawlensky ended his search for perfection in 1936 with his series of "Meditations." The face has been reduced to its most essential components. One can imagine Jawlensky's personal agony as each determined, precise brushstroke reflects his own arthritic pain. Yet his framework resembles the form of the Eastern Orthodox cross, reflecting his personal devotion and strength: "To suffer incessantly is very hard," he wrote. "The pain doesn't let me move....I just sit and work...I work for myself and for my God. But my work is my prayer, an impassioned prayer spoken in colors."[11]

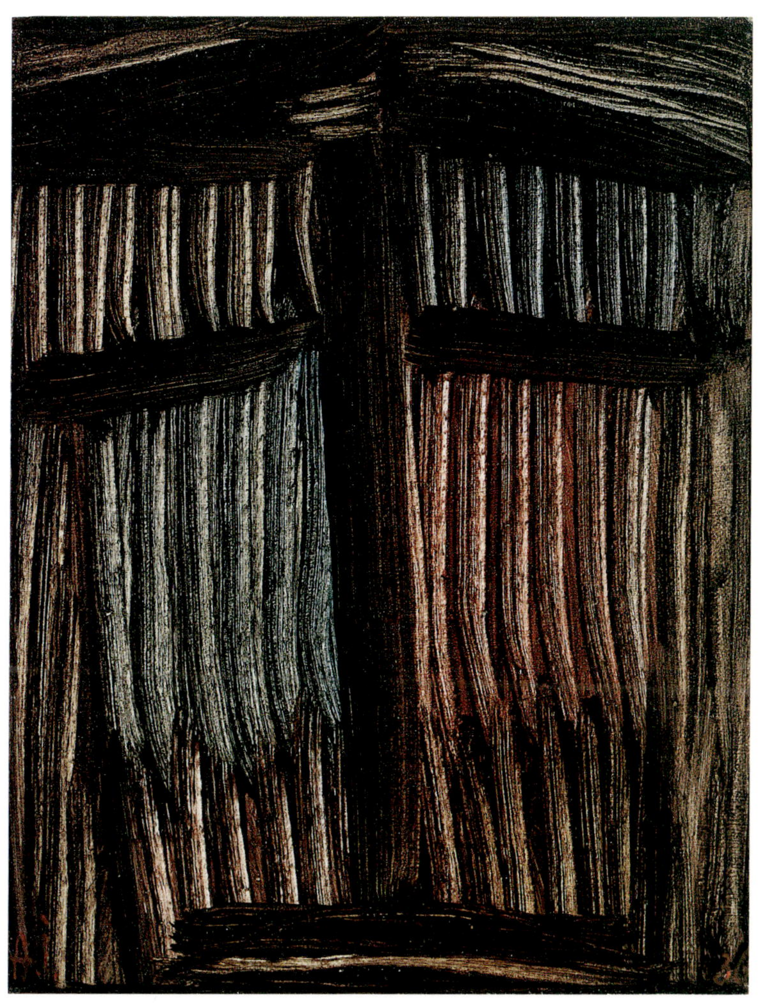

NOTES

[1] Clemens Weiler, *Alexei Jawlensky* (Koln: M. DuMont Schauberg, 1959), p. 17.

[2] Peg Weiss, *Kandinsky in Munich* (Princeton: Princeton University Press, 1979), pp. 13–16.

[3] Franz Marc, "The 'Savages' of Germany," *The Blaue Reiter Almanac,* Documentary Edition edited by Klaus Lankheit (New York: The Viking Press, 1974), p. 64.

[4] "Alexej Jawlensky an P. Willibrord Verkade," *Das Kunstwerk* II, nos. 1–2, p. 49.

[5] Letter from Jawlensky to Galka Scheyer, February 23, 1935. Unless otherwise noted, the correspondence cited is in the collection of the Blue Four Galka Scheyer Archives, Norton Simon Museum.

[6] Undated letter from Jawlensky to Scheyer, November 1918.

[7] Undated letter from Jawlensky to Scheyer, December 1920.

[8] Letter from Jawlensky to Scheyer, October 11, 1920.

[9] Letter from Jawlensky to Father Willibrord Verkade, June 12, 1938, published in Clemens Weiler, *Jawlensky Heads Faces Meditations* (New York: Praeger Publishers Inc., 1971), p. 108.

[10] Letter from Jawlensky to Scheyer, January 3, 1936.

[11] Letter from Jawlensky to Scheyer, May 12, 1936.

Published by
NORTON SIMON MUSEUM
411 West Colorado Boulevard
Pasadena, California 91105

ISBN 0-915776-06-5
Library of Congress Catalog
Card No. 90-63306
Printed in Japan

Designed by Lilli Cristin
Photography by Antoni Dolinski

Front cover:
LIFE AND DEATH, 1923
Oil on cardboard, 16⅞ x 12⅞"